Till death do us part

Till death do us part

The Secret to Making Marriage Work

Patrick J. Ruffin

Columbus, Ohio

Till Death Do Us Part: The Secret to Making Marriage Work

Published by Gatekeeper Press
2167 Stringtown Rd, Suite 109
Columbus, OH 43123-2989
www.GatekeeperPress.com

Copyright © 2021 by Patrick J. Ruffin

All rights reserved. Neither this book, nor any parts within it may be sold or reproduced in any form or by any electronic or mechanical means, including information storage and retrieval systems without permission in writing from the author. The only exception is by a reviewer, who may quote short excerpts in a review.

Cover Image Copyright: iStockphoto.com/bonetta

Library of Congress Control Number: 2020952271

ISBN (paperback): 9781662907975
eISBN: 9781662906800

Bible quotations fall under "Gratis Use" or "Public Domain" fair use and are taken from various versions:

- (AMP) Scripture quotations marked (AMP) are taken from the Amplified Bible, Copyright © 1954, 1958, 1962, 1964, 1965, 1987 by The Lockman Foundation. Used by permission.

- (KJV) Scripture quotations from The Authorized (King James) Version. Rights in the Authorized Version in the United Kingdom are vested in the Crown. Reproduced by permission of the Crown's patentee, Cambridge University Press

- (NIrV) Scriptures taken from the Holy Bible, New International Reader's Version®, NIrV® Copyright © 1995, 1996, 1998, 2014 by Biblica, Inc.®Used by permission of Zondervan. www.zondervan.com The "NIrV" and "New International Reader's Version" are trademarks registered in the United States Patent and Trademark Office by Biblica, Inc.®

- (NIV) Scriptures taken from the Holy Bible, New International Version®, NIV®. Copyright © 1973, 1978, 1984, 2011 by Biblica, Inc.™ Used by permission of Zondervan. All rights reserved worldwide. www.zondervan.com The "NIV" and "New International Version" are trademarks registered in the United States Patent and Trademark Office by Biblica, Inc.®

- (NLT) Scripture quotations marked (NLT) are taken from the Holy Bible, New Living Translation, copyright ©1996, 2004, 2015 by Tyndale House Foundation. Used by permission of Tyndale House Publishers, Carol Stream, Illinois 60188. All rights reserved.

- (NKJV) Scripture taken from the New King James Version®. Copyright © 1982 by Thomas Nelson. Used by permission. All rights reserved.

- (NRSV) Common Bible: New Revised Standard Version Bible, copyright 1989, Division of Christian Education of the National Council of the Churches of Christ in the United States of America. Used by permission. All rights reserved.

DEDICATION

I would like to dedicate this book to my Lord and Savior, Jesus Christ, who has changed my life. Also, to my beautiful, lovely, and gorgeous wife Pamela, whom I love dearly, and to my two awesome children, Brianna and Benjamin.

CONTENTS

	ACKNOWLEDGMENTS	i
I	PATRICK & PAM PRINCIPLES: "MARRIAGE TAKES WORK"	1
II	PURPOSE & PLAN FOR MARRIAGE	13
III	PRAY TOGETHER	27
IV	PRAISE & WORSHIP TOGETHER	35
V	PLAY TOGETHER	43
VI	PROCLAIM THE PROMISE TOGETHER	55
VII	TILL DEATH DO US PART	73
	ABOUT THE AUTHOR	75
	Endnotes	76

ACKNOWLEDGMENTS

Jesus Christ can make a difference in your life and in your marriage.

I

PATRICK & PAM PRINCIPLES: "MARRIAGE TAKES WORK"

Good marriages do not happen by chance or by happenstance. To have a good marriage, you must work at it. It takes a conscious decision to decide that I am going to do whatever it takes to make this marriage work. Marriage is like anything in life: The more you work at it, the better it gets.

It is interesting how many people are more concerned about the success of their sports team than the success of their marriage. Amazingly, many put more effort into taking care of their cars than taking care of their spouses. It is incredible that we walk our dogs daily, but we rarely walk with our spouses. To make a marriage successful, it will take work.

When I first got married, I thought that all I needed to do was "bring home the bacon" and all would be well. Yet I found out that my wife wanted more than the bacon; she wanted to spend time with the one who brought home the bacon. She wanted to experience life with the one who brought home the bacon. Having a successful marriage takes hard work, but in the end, it is worth it.

There is an attack on marriage. However, I have found out that having Jesus in your marriage will make a difference in your marriage.

There is an attack on marriage, especially biblical marriage. The enemy wants to destroy the institution of biblical marriage because it reflects the relationship God has with the church.

The enemy wants us to think that a relationship without a spouse is faulty, just as our relationship with God is faulty. Even so, marriage is God ordained, and what God has put together, let no man, woman, or demonic presence put asunder.

First of all, we must remember that marriage is ordained and created by God.

"So God created man in his own image, in the image of God he created him; male and female he created them. And God blessed them. And God said to them, 'Be fruitful and multiply and fill the earth'." (Genesis 1:27-28, NKJV)

Whatever God made is good, and that includes marriage. Many people refuse to commit to marriage because they "love evil rather than good." They love to live outside the bounds of what God has said was good.

God in 1 Corinthians 7:1-2 (AMP) says that in order **"to avoid sexual immorality, let each man have his own wife, and let each woman have her own husband."** In other words, I have my own and you have your own; you leave mine alone and I will leave yours alone. There is no place like home when you have your own.

Sexual expression is only good with God within the confines of marriage. The above scripture says in **"let every man/woman have their own wife/husband."** It does not say have your own girlfriend/boyfriend, partner, lover, beau, companion, soul mate, steady flame, sweetheart, or a friend with benefits.

I once heard a good saying, that boys play house but men get married. There is a lot of truth to that statement. Many people's lives are like the former Toys "R" Us slogan: "I Don't Wanna Grow Up."

A lot of males/females are not getting married because they still have the little boy/little girl in them, and they still want to play house. Many want the benefits of marriage (sex, financial fulfillment, children), but they do not want to commit to being married.

I am the "Voice of Experience" in this area. I dated my wife for seven years, not because I did not love her, not because she wasn't a perfect fit for me, not because she wasn't extremely beautiful, lovely and gorgeous (she was, and she still is).

I did not want to get married because I was still a little boy and the little boy in me did not want to commit to a lasting marriage. The scripture says in 1 Corinthians 13:11 (AMP), **"When I was a child, I talked like a child, I thought like a child, I reasoned like a child; when I became a man, I did away with childish things."** I was a terrible boyfriend, but I am a man now, and I am making up for the lost time by being the best husband of all time.

Many men/women need to stop "shacking up" (old-school lingo) and just grow up, fess up to God, and get hitched up in marriage. Then they will see the blessings of God poured out and upon them.

Many fail to realize that abundant blessings come when we are obedient to living life God's way and not our own way. For example, when God created marriage, he created it as a lifelong commitment.

Divorce is not in God's plan, but as Jesus mentioned in Matthew 19:8 (KJV), it was allowed **"because of the hardness of their hearts."** He did not plan it but permitted it.

Divorce is devastating to the individual, families, and to society, especially when children are involved. I have personally witnessed the aftermath of divorce in my own family, in my church, and amongst my friends.

Sue Schlesman, a Christian writer, teacher, blogger, and speaker once wrote about the "*Ten Hidden Consequences of Divorce.*"[1] This is what she wrote:

1. Grief

Divorce is a death of a union, and therefore the death of a dream, a promise, a life, and a family unit. Everyone involved—even a perpetrator—will feel grief and loss during a divorce.

2. Trauma

Divorce marks a pivotal moment in a person's life, especially for children; life as they know it changes forever and they become different versions of themselves, adapting to new routines and new versions of their parents (who have also changed). They might move to a new home, new school, or be a part of a new step-family. Often, children take responsibility for their parents' divorce, internalizing guilt and regret over the break-up. Even normalizing the widespread acceptance of divorce and step-families in our culture can't diminish a child's trauma at losing his/her parent from the home, especially to someone else like a new wife or step-child. (55 percent of divorcees will remarry.)

3. Relationship with the Ex-Spouse

Couples get divorced because they want to stop talking, problem-solving, and living with their spouse. However, if they have kids, not only do they have to stay in contact with one another, but their communications skills (which were bad before) actually must improve. Parents must still work together to solve problems concerning their children, which now involve a tug-of-war over time, money, influence, gifts, vacations, etc. And to make things harder, there will likely be new spouses influencing these decisions. Parents still have to figure out how to get along.

4. Financial Stress

The average divorce proceeding in America costs between $15,000-$20,000, plus relocation and replacement expenses after the household items are divided up. In addition to child/spousal support, two households typically require double bedrooms, vacations, toys, and clothes for the kids who travel back and forth between their parents: it's more money out of both parents' pockets. Unfortunately, the average single mother earns only $36,700 per year.

5. Emotional Problems

Following a divorce, parents and children often experience emotional problems that can last for years, even for the rest of their lives. Anxiety, depression, fear of abandonment, distrust, insecurity, lack of intimacy, confusion over sexuality and/or gender, guilt, avoidance of conflict, faithlessness, control, loneliness, bitterness, and rebellion manifest themselves in children who have lived through a parents' divorce.

6. The Chance of Another Divorce

60 percent of divorcees who remarry will divorce again; third marriages dissolve 93 percent of the time. Why? Perhaps people don't work on their issues; perhaps they're too busy trying to survive. Realistically, most people carry their issues into the next marriage (along with the new baggage from their last divorce). Very often, people are also attracted to the same type of person as they were before.

7. Losing Friends

Most divorced people, while they remain single, eventually find new single friends. At some point, they begin to feel awkward in their previous married friends' circles. Divorcees also lose married friends if those friends feel pressured to choose sides; they may choose one spouse over the other, or they may jettison from both friendships to avoid further conflict.

8. Dividing of Memories and Belongings

While household items and family photos don't hold a lot of intrinsic value, dividing them between parents can be heart-wrenching because household items represent memories and commitment. Family photos capture times of love and unity that can be both painful and precious. Just like going through the belongings of a parent who's died, dividing up a household between spouses (or even if one person keeps it all) brings feelings of heartache, resentment, and regret.

9. Holidays

Divorced parents will have to share the kids on holidays or rotate holidays. Either way, that leaves one parent alone or without their kids on some of the most sentimental and nostalgic days of the year. Other important days, like graduations, birthdays, and weddings become events that must be shared by both parents simultaneously, which can create tension if the exes have not figured out how to be cordial to one another and one another's new spouses (if they exist). A lifetime of uncomfortable holidays is not something most people want.

10. Singleness

Singles comprise 43 percent of America's adults. If you're in a bad marriage, singleness looks attractive. But once you've been married and you find yourself divorced, you probably aren't so comfortable back out there in the dating world. Divorcees must navigate singleness very carefully, especially if they have kids. Without another parent in the home, single parents tend to rely heavily on neighbors, boyfriends/girlfriends, and extended family to babysit when they can't be home. Another caution here is dating itself—having a potential new mom or dad in and out of the house is emotionally confusing and traumatizing for kids. If you date with kids in the house, be wary of exposure and attachment until you feel confident about the security of the relationship. Children of divorce are especially susceptible to feeling abandoned and unwanted. You might consider remaining single until the kids are grown.

I agree with Sue Schlesman's assessment of divorce. When contemplating divorce one must add up the cost. The cost of divorce may impart a lasting impression for generations to come.

God's plan for the family was that one man and one woman would commit themselves to each other for life, and for them to live happily ever after until He calls them home to Glory.

But it takes work to go from "I do" to "happily ever after." In this book, I will discuss how to get to the "happily ever after." This book is based on twenty-nine years of trial and error. I wish I'd had a book like this while dating and contemplating marriage. It would have helped us get through many of the storms of dating.

I tell those who were married and got a divorce that if your first marriage didn't work out, there is no need to be disheartened because we serve a God who offers another chance.

The Lord is concerned with what you are going to do from this day forward, not with what has been done in the past. The past is the past; you cannot change what has already been done. But what are you going to do now?

The scripture (John 8:3-11, KJV) tells us about a group of scribes and Pharisees who caught a woman in the act of adultery. They asked Jesus what He was going to do about it, because the punishment for someone like her should be stoning as prescribed by the Mosaic Law. Jesus told them that the one who is without sin should cast the first stone.

All the men started to walk away, starting from the oldest to the youngest. You see, the oldest had been living the longest, and it did not take them long to remember their many past sins.

After the men left, Jesus said something to the woman that was unexpected. He asked where her accusers were and told her, "Neither do I condemn you." Yet witness what Jesus said after this statement.

He didn't tell the woman next time pull down her blinds. He didn't tell her what you are doing is "OK" because all of us have wants, needs, and urges. He didn't tell her to make sure she used protection. He didn't tell her next time make sure she locks her bedroom door. No, He told her to "Go, and sin no more." Go and get out of the sin business. Make a change from this day forward.

What the Lord wants us to do for those who have gotten a divorce is the same as the woman who was caught in adultery. He does not want us to condemn and stone those who have gotten a divorce. Yes, many have gotten a divorce for many different reasons. However, what the Lord is telling those who have gotten a divorce is that when/if you get married again, go and divorce no more — that you will no longer be known as a divorcee, but as someone who is now faithful to their wedding vows.

I have married many couples and have done pre-marital counseling and post-marital counseling. Some of these couples have wonderful marriages and others do not. For years I wondered what made my marriage different from other marriages. Why are we enjoying a joyful marriage when other marriages are full of fuming, fighting, cussing, and cutting?

Through the years, my wife and I have seen many of our friends and families get married and have attended and participated in several elaborate wedding ceremonies.

However, we have also witnessed several of these couples get a divorce. I always thought to myself, why would a loving couple spend hundreds or even thousands of dollars on a wedding, standing at the altar before friends, family, and God to say "I do" but in a few short years say "I do" again, but not with you.

These divorces occurred from those that are both outside and within the church. Yes, we have personally known church laypersons, deacons, ministers, preachers, pastors, apostles, teachers, and musicians who have gotten divorced.

I always wondered, with all these divorces in and outside of the church, what are we doing right? You see, I'm not the perfect man — I have faults, I have issues, I have days that make me want to holler and throw up both my hands.

I have days where I don't want to be bothered by anyone, not my church members, not my bishop, not my neighbors, not my friends, not my family, including my children — and not even my wife. My wife Pam is beautiful, gorgeous, and lovely. She is the ideal wife and mother. She is always concerned about others rather than herself, but she is still not perfect, and, yes, there have been days, although not many, that she has gotten on my last nerve. You see, that is what happens when two imperfect people get together. Yes, like all of us, at times both of us **"have sinned, and come short of the glory of God."** (Romans 3:23, KJV)

The scriptures say in Ecclesiastes 7:20 (NRSV), **"Surely there is no one on earth so righteous as to do good without ever sinning."** We are naturally born sinners.

Yet even in our humanness, we are still committed to the marriage. We have decided to stick it out "for better, for worse." I told my wife that if she decides to leave me for some insane reason, I will be going with her. I would be a fool to leave her, and she would be a fool to leave me. We are committed to the marriage no matter what.

However, just because you say you want to stay together and are committed to staying together does not mean it is going to happen. In other words, a good marriage takes work; you must work to keep it together. Being happily married just does not happen by chance. You and your spouse must work at it daily, weekly, monthly, and yearly.

So for twenty-eight years, my wife and I have been working at it — working to stay together, working to love one another, working to be there for each other. We have been working on doing four key things in our marriage.

We have incorporated four principles and practices into our marriage, and they keep us tighter. These are four things that solidify the marriage, four procedures that have kept us grounded through the thick and the thin, and four things that are non-negotiable. These are four things that we will not bend or break, and because of these four things, our marriage has been solid.

Our marriage has been centered on four things. We do one thing every day, one thing once a week, one thing once a month, and lastly, there is something we do every year.

Here is our secret, it's simple but profound. We **Pray** every day, we **Praise** and worship together every week, we **Play** purposely every month, and every year we keep our **Promise** and celebrate publicly to continue to stay as husband and wife.

For the remainder of this book, I will go into detail as to what Pray, Praise, Play, and Promise look like. I will share the successes and failures of us trying to live out what we have promised to do.

I challenge any couple — those who are thinking about marriage, those who are newly married, and those who are seasoned in their marriage — to incorporate these four things, and not only will your relationship become better, but it will also blossom.

My wife and I do not have the perfect marriage; we are two imperfect people striving together and loving one another with the help of the Lord. The scriptures ask the question in Amos 3:3 (NKJV), **"Can two walk together, unless they are agreed?"** I like the Amplified version of Amos 3:3 (AMP), that says, **"Do two men walk together unless they have made an appointment?"** In other words, if you have not made an appointment to walk together with someone, you will be walking alone.

My wife and I have made an appointment — an agreement to walk through life together. I am not walking alone, and she is not walking alone. But the key to our marriage is that as a couple we are not walking alone; we have Jesus walking with us. You can walk with someone without agreeing, but it won't be fun. It will feel more like a burden rather than a blessing.

The book of Ecclesiastes 4:12 (AMP) tells us, **"A cord of three strands is not quickly broken."** Jesus is the third cord in our marriage and because of Him, nothing will be able to tear us apart.

Without the help of the Lord, our marriage would not be what it is.

Yes, marriage takes work, but the work is worth it in the end.

II

PURPOSE & PLAN FOR MARRIAGE

What is the purpose and plan for marriage? Why even get married? If you're happy all by yourself, why even consider it? If you want to be intimate with one partner or several partners of the opposite sex or even the same sex, and it feels good, why should you get married? Why even consider being in a husband-and-wife, committed marriage relationship for life?

You have seen couples get married and then divorce, why would you want to put yourself through that pain and anguish? Life is too short. Why don't you just live it up and commit to the three most important people in your life — me, myself, and I?

Yes, we have heard all these arguments about marriage, but before we get into the pros and cons of being in a married relationship, let us remember that marriage is not man-made, it's God-made. Marriage is an institution that was set forth by God and qualified by Jesus.

Author Tim Keller said, "Men will never be a good groom to their wife unless they first be a good bride to Jesus. A successful marriage requires falling in love many times, always with the same person, Jesus."[2]

God established marriage and His word regarding being in a long-term, committed, husband-and-wife relationship supersedes anything that is written by Dr. Phil or advice given on *Iyanla, Fix My Life*.

God's word is the final book of arbitration. We should go by what God has said. If you are a follower of Jesus Christ, the buck stops with the Bible. If you are not a follower of Jesus Christ, getting your marriage together should not be your top priority. Your top priority should be to get right with God.

Jesus said in Mark 8:36 (NKJV), **"For what will it profit a man if he gains the whole world, and loses his own soul?"** What would it profit you to have a perfect marriage, but lose your soul? The most important thing for you to do is to **"seek first his kingdom and His righteousness,"** as Jesus said in Matthew 6:33 (NKJV). If you are reading this, and you are not right with God, today is your day, this hour is your hour. You are not reading this by mistake or by luck. This is a divine appointment.

Here is how you get right with God. First, you must know what God has said about sin. The scripture in Romans 3:23 (NKJV) says, **"for all have sinned and fall short of the glory of God."** To get right with God, we must first realize that we are sinners, and our sin separates us from God.

According to the scriptures, even on our best day without Christ in our life, all of us are torn up from the floor up. You are no good. I am no good. Romans 3:10 (NKJV) says, **"There is none righteous, no, not one."** You may think that you are not included in that statement, but according to God's holy standards, you still miss the mark. It takes only one sin to deem you unfit for Heaven. It takes only one sin to send you to Hell. The scriptures say in Romans 6:23 (NKJV), **"For the wages of sin is death. . . ."** Sin is a killer. It will kill you mentally, spiritually, physically, and eventually, eternally if you do not get right with God.

However, in our wretched condition, there is hope. We have hope in God expressed through Jesus Christ. The hope is found in Romans 5:8 (NKJV), **"But God demonstrates His own love toward us, in that while we were still sinners, Christ died for us."** Yes, Jesus died for you although you are in your mess — although you are doing everything that you are big and bad enough to do. While you are sinning and grinning, Jesus died for your sins. But he was raised to be your Savior. No one else could or would do it for you, and no other religion can say this. Neither Judaism, Hinduism, Buddhism, nor Islam can make this claim.

Once you come into the realization that you are a sinner and Jesus is your only Savior, to get right with God, you must respond by calling out to Jesus to save you from your sins. Romans 10:9-10 (NIV) tells us, **"If you declare with your mouth, 'Jesus is Lord,' and believe in your heart that God raised him from the dead, you will be saved. For it is with your heart that you believe and are justified, and it is with your mouth that you profess your faith and are saved."**

Jesus is willing to save you if you accept the free gift of salvation. The scripture tells us in Romans 10:13 (NIV), **". . . 'Everyone who calls on the name of the Lord will be saved'."** If you put your trust in Jesus, He will save you. He will save you from the power of sin, the punishment of sin, and the very presence of sin one day. Hallelujah!

Now that you have given your life to Christ, you can rejoice in your salvation and have peace with God. Romans 5:1-2 (NIV) states, **"Therefore, since we have been justified through faith, we have peace with God through our Lord Jesus Christ, through whom we have gained access by faith into this grace in which we now stand."** Being saved gives you access to God. Now that you have access to God, you can now go to the Lord and ask Him for help with your marriage. The scriptures in Psalms 46:1 (NIV) state, **"God is our refuge and strength, a very present help in trouble."** If you are having trouble in your marriage, God is the one to go to.

If you are having marriage difficulties, you can now talk to a friend. The best friend to talk to is Jesus. He is no longer a stranger but a friend.

As a child of God, you are no longer condemned; you can now be in right relationships with people because you are right with God. Romans 8:1 (NIV) tells us, **"Therefore, there is now no condemnation for those who are in Christ Jesus."** Because of Jesus, you now have a future and hope.

When I was dating my girlfriend, who is now my wife, I was not saved. I did not have a personal relationship with Jesus. I was in the house of God, but I was not in the church of God. However, when I gave my life to Christ before getting married, it totally changed my life and has made a major difference in my marriage. The scriptures are right. 2 Corinthians 5:17 (NIV) states, **"Therefore, if anyone is in Christ, he is a new creature; the old things passed away; behold, new things have come. The old has gone, the new is here."** My life was so radically changed that my wife also gave her life to Christ. As my mother used to say, "Look at God!"

Once you get right with God, then he can help you with your marriage. *Focus on the Family* states the following about Christian marriages:

> "The divorce rates of Christian believers are not identical to the general population – not even close. Being a committed, faithful believer makes a measurable difference in marriage. Saying you believe something or merely belonging to a church, unsurprisingly, does little for your marriage. But the more you are involved in the actual practice of your faith in real ways – through submitting yourself to a serious body of believers, regularly learning from scripture, being in communion with God through prayer individually and with your spouse and children, and having friends and family around us who challenge us to take our marriages seriously – the greater difference this makes

in strengthening both the quality and longevity of our marriages. Faith does matter and the leading sociologists of family and religion tell us so."[3]

So, what is the purpose of marriage? Let me first dispel a myth. The overall purpose of marriage is not to make you happy. The overall purpose of marriage is to glorify God. Pastor Rick Warren in an article entitled "*The Purpose-Driven Marriage*"[4] states, "Our main purpose in marriage should be greater than fulfilling our own wants and needs or even the wants and needs of our spouse. Our main purpose in marriage should be to focus on being of the same mind, according to Jesus, so that with one accord and one voice, we glorify God." What Pastor Warren is saying is that marriage is not about you, but it is all about God. How can I please God? Our goal is to please God in both our singleness and our marriage.

Author, Julie Kloster writes in her book *Glorify God Together: A Marriage of Purpose* [5] about four major points of marriage:

1. The marriage relationship teaches us to have authentic and intimate fellowship and a strong sense of community with all believers.
2. God uses the marriage relationship to make us more like Christ.
3. God uses the marriage relationship to train us to honor and serve others above ourselves.
4. Marriage may give us a partner to help spread the gospel of Christ.

If you and your spouse are followers of Jesus Christ, he/she is also your brother and sister in Christ.

You and your spouse are a force to be reckoned with. You and your spouse are a threat to the enemy. That is why Satan wants to tear Christian marriages apart. He knows what two committed Christians can do for the cause of Christ.

He knows that two Christ-dedicated people in a committed husband/wife Christian relationship can do damage to the Kingdom of Satan, especially in raising children in a God-fearing household, where they make the proclamation in Joshua 24:15 (KJV), **"As for me and my house, we will serve the Lord."** When they raised their children to do the same, that is how the Gospel of Jesus Christ went forward for generations to come.

That is why the Devil does not want to see you and your spouse commit to "Till Death Do Us Part."

Marriage was started with and instituted by God in His word. God instituted marriage in Genesis 2:24 (NKJV), saying, **"Therefore a man shall leave his father and his mother and be joined to his wife, and they shall become one flesh."**

The biblical definition of marriage is one man and one woman in a committed, God-fearing relationship for life.

Paul said in 1 Corinthians 7:2 (NKJV), **"let each man have his own wife, and let each woman have her own husband."** Each man should have his own wife. It does not say that each man should have his own boyfriend/ girlfriend, partner, sweetheart, lover, baby mama, friend, or friend with benefits.

Also, it says in the same verse, **"let every woman have her own husband."** It does not say let every woman have her own girlfriend/ boyfriend, sugar daddy, beau, boo, or squeeze. There is a difference in these relationships from being a husband or wife, both biblically and spiritually.

If you want your marriage to work, it is best to learn from the best-selling book of all time, the Bible. God's word has the final authority on everything pertaining to marriage.

One of my favorite marriage scriptures is Proverbs 18:22 (NKJV), **"He who finds a wife finds a good thing and obtains favor from the Lord."**

I found my good thing and I am staying with my good thing. Because by me finding my good thing and being committed to my good thing for life, I have obtained favor from the Lord. Don't you want to have the favor of God, then get married and stay married?

Another one of my favorite marriage scriptures is 1 Corinthians 7:2-4 (NKJV), **"Nevertheless, because of sexual immorality, let each man have his own wife, and let each woman have her own husband. But because of immoralities, each man is to have his own wife, and each woman is to have her own husband. The husband must fulfill his duty to his wife, and likewise also the wife to her husband. The wife does not have authority over her own body, but the husband does; and likewise also the husband does not have authority over his own body, but the wife does. Stop depriving one another, except by agreement for a time, so that you may devote yourselves to prayer, and come together again so that Satan will not tempt you because of your lack of self-control."**

I have my own wife; you have your own wife. You leave mine alone, and I will leave yours alone. It is good to come home to someone who is yours and yours alone. It is my duty to take care of my wife's sexual needs, and it is her duty to take care of mine. If you are not in a mutually agreed-upon prayer meeting, you should be in a mutually agreed-upon session "in between the sheets," because that is what the scripture says. God's word is the best word. God's word is better than any sex counselor. God's word makes it good to be married.

My all-time favorite marriage scripture is Hebrews 13:4 (NKJV), **"Marriage is honorable among all, and the bed undefiled; but fornicators and adulterers God will judge."**

Being married and staying married is honorable. Anything done in the bed between you and your spouse that is not harmful, sinful, or degrading is undefiled and honorable. You and your spouse can swing from the chandelier if you like. That is OK with God.

However, anything done in the bed outside of marriage is dishonorable. It is dishonorable to the man, it is dishonorable to the woman, but most importantly, it is dishonorable to God. If you have children, it is dishonorable to the children. God did not call you to be a baby mama or a baby daddy; God loves you too much for that. He has a better way for you, which is found in a committed husband-and-wife relationship.

Sex is the representation of the celebration of two people committed to one another and to God. This should be a regular practice of those in a one-man-one-woman, committed, consensual marriage relationship.

According to scripture, not everyone should be having sex.

Which type of sexual relationship does God condone and which ones does he condemn? Can you pass God's sex test? Which relationship are you in?

1. One man and one woman in a committed, consensual, marital relationship.

2. One man and one woman in a committed, consensual, non-marital relationship.

3. One man and one woman in a non-committed, consensual, non-marital relationship.

4. One man and one woman in a non-committed, non-consensual, non-marital relationship.

5. One man and one man in a committed, consensual, marital relationship.

6. One man and one man in a committed, consensual, non-marital relationship.

7. One man and one man in a non-committed, consensual, non-marital relationship.

8. One man and one man in a non-committed, non-consensual, non-marital relationship.

9. One woman and one woman in a committed, consensual, marital relationship.

10. One woman and one woman in a committed, consensual, non-marital relationship.

11. One woman and one woman in a non-committed, consensual, non-marital relationship.

12. One woman and one woman in a non-committed, non-consensual, non-marital relationship.

There are at least twelve or more different sexual relations you can have with a partner. Out of the twelve, there is only one that is blessed by God. Only one is considered sacred by God. Which one are you in? Did you pass God's sex test?

I am not hating on anyone, because before I gave my life to Jesus Christ, I was guilty of many of the same sins.

However, the buck stops with the Bible. God has the final say.

God's word is true even if you do not believe it, accept it, or want to live by it. God will not change His truth to suit our pleasures nor will He wink at sin. At the end of the day, we all must answer to God.

The Word of the Bible says in Romans 3:4 (NIV) **"Let God be true, and every human being a liar."**

The scriptures speak loudly against sex outside of a husband-and-wife committed relationship.

- 1 Corinthians 6:18 (NIV) — "Flee from sexual immorality. All other sins a person commits are outside the body, but whoever sins sexually, sins against their own body."

- 1 Thessalonians 4:3-5 (NIV) — "It is God's will that you should be sanctified: that you should avoid sexual immorality; that each of you should learn to control your own body in a way that is holy and honorable, not in passionate lust like the pagans, who do not know God."

- Matthew 5:28 (NIV) — "But I tell you that anyone who looks at a woman lustfully has already committed adultery with her in his heart."

- 1 Corinthians 6:9 (NIV) — "Or do you not know that wrongdoers will not inherit the kingdom of God? Do not be deceived: Neither the sexually immoral nor idolaters nor adulterers nor men who have sex with men."

- Ephesians 5:3 (NIV) — "But among you there must not be even a hint of sexual immorality, or of any kind of impurity, or of greed, because these are improper for God's holy people."

- Leviticus 18:22 (NIV) — "'Do not have sexual relations with a man as one does with a woman; that is detestable."

- 1 Corinthians 7:9 (NIV) — "But if they cannot control themselves, they should marry, for it is better to marry than to burn with passion."

Love should be the number one reason you get married, and that means love for your significant other but most importantly love for God. You want to do right by God.

About nine-in-ten Americans (88 percent) cited love as a very important reason to get married, ahead of making a lifelong commitment (81 percent) and companionship (76 percent), according to a 2013 Pew Research Center survey.[6]

This scripture is telling us that if you love your boyfriend/girlfriend so much that you cannot live without them, you cannot keep your hands off of them, and you feel that you got to have it, it is biblical to do what Beyoncé sings about. "Put a Ring on It"[7] and go to the justice and get some peace. Get married and stop burning in your lust.

People should not believe the hype that marriage is not for them. But even statistics say that life is better in a committed Christian marriage than experiencing life in a relationship without a committed Christian marriage.

God's plan is the right plan.

Dr. Brad Wilcox, director of the National Marriage Project, states that "Active conservative protestants who attend church regularly are actually 35% less likely to divorce than those who have no religious preferences." [8]

In an article, Shaunti Feldhahn states, "The studies show that if couples stay married for five years, that almost 80 percent of those will be happy five years later."[9]

Robert H. Shmerling, MD, Senior Faculty Editor, Harvard Health Publishing, states the following:[10]

- Your behavior improves with marriage. Married people may take fewer risks, eat better, and maintain healthier lifestyles, on average, compared with single people.

- Mental health is better when you're married. Poor social supports (as might be more likely for those who are single) have been strongly linked with higher rates of depression, loneliness, and social isolation, which have in turn been associated with poorer health outcomes.

- Married people have better health before getting married. It's reasonable to wonder whether people with medical problems (or who are prone to them due to unhealthy habits) are less likely to get married; that would leave healthier people getting married, and that could account for the "marriage health benefit." But some studies have actually found that unhealthy men tend to marry at a younger age and divorce less often than healthy men.

"Previous studies have found that married persons have lower mortality rates than unmarried persons, attributable to either selectivity in entering marriage (i.e., healthier people are more likely to marry) or health-protective effects of marriage, or a combination of the two.[11]

If you want to be happy, if you want to be healthier, it is better that you marry instead of burning in your lust. So, for the remainder of this book, I'm going to break down the principles my wife and I have been abiding by for (at the time of this writing in 2020) twenty-nine years.

I will give you four solid steps that you can apply to set your marriage on the path of "Till Death Do Us Part." If you and your spouse faithfully commit your marriage to these four steps, your marriage will not only improve, it will be fabulous. In your marriage you will experience greater satisfaction and fulfilment.

Let us examine the four steps that will keep your marriage thriving.

Let us start with Prayer.

III

PRAY TOGETHER
"THE FAMILY THAT PRAYS TOGETHER STAYS TOGETHER."

This statement is so profoundly true. A family that reaches out to God for help, for guidance, and for security becomes closer to each other and to God, but I would like to take it even further. The marriage that prays together stays together.

One of the key ingredients to keeping a marriage together is simply praying daily with your spouse. It doesn't have to be fifteen minutes of anointing-of-oil, laying-of-hands, slaying-in-the-spirit praying. It may be just a one-to-two-minute prayer in the morning or in the afternoon, just joining together, thanking God for being together, and partitioning for breakthroughs, deliverance, and miracles.

It is very difficult to pray and fuss at the same time. I remember a time in which my wife and I were having an intense dispute. I do not remember what the discussion was about, but I do remember that both of us were quite passionate about our own point of view.

Since it was our custom to pray, I told her, "Let's pray about it." Well, she was not in the mood to pray, and I was not in the mood to pray, but we prayed anyway, and somehow God worked the problem out. It is amazing what happens when we are obedient to God's word.

The scripture tells us in 1 Thessalonians 5:16-18 (NIV), **"Rejoice always, pray continually, give thanks in all circumstances; for this is God's will for you in Christ Jesus."**

If couples would just use this scripture as their "life verse," there would be less stress and turmoil in the marriage.

Paul, the writer of this text, is telling us to rejoice always. Always means always. Rejoice when your spouse does not wash the dishes in the sink or make up the bed. Rejoice when dinner is not cooked the way your mommy used to cook it. Rejoice when your spouse doesn't know the meaning of saving and never found a sale he/she didn't like. We should rejoice just to know that God has sent you someone to share your life. If you cannot find anything to rejoice in, rejoice in that.

Then Paul continues in 1 Thessalonians 5:17 (NIV), **"Pray continually."** In other words, do not stop praying. Prayer should be more than something that we do, it should be who we are. We should always be in a posture of prayer. Consistent and regular prayer is the glue that keeps marriage intact.

Praying is something that most couples do not do regularly.

However, a *Time Magazine* study even said that praying is beneficial to the relationship:

> **Pray for their partner:** *Yep, prayer. Several peer-reviewed studies published in respected journals suggest that praying for your partner*

makes relationships last. "The guys who are doing this work are pretty well-known in the relationship realm and are not at religious institutions," says Ogolsky. "If you've had asked me what I thought about this five years ago, I would have said 'ah no.' This is not one of the things I would have ever thought would have been quite as robust as it is." Apart from the supernatural explanation, prayer might work like mindfulness, or help the person doing the praying to think compassionately about their partner.[12]

When a couple prays together, what they are saying is that they are turning to someone bigger than themselves to handle the issues of life. Prayer allows the couple to share what is in their hearts without directly speaking to the other person. If you can pray about it, it makes it easier to talk about it.

A lot of men — that includes me — do not want to ask for help. Most men try to figure it out on their own before asking for help, but to showcase your heart to your wife, it is wise to openly pray about your fears. God can handle our fears. There is power in praying together. The scriptures say in Matthew 18:20 (NIV), **"For where two or three gather in my name, there am I with them."** It just takes you and your spouse to have church. It takes you and your spouse just touching and agreeing in prayer for God to move on your behalf.

Jesus said in Matthew 18:19 (AMP), **"Again I say to you, that if two [a] believers on earth agree [that is, are of one mind, in harmony] about anything that they ask [within the will of God], it will be done for them by My Father in heaven."** The enemy does not want you to pray together because he knows what will happen.

- The scripture tells us in James 5:16 (AMP), "Therefore, confess your sins to one another [your false steps, your offenses], and pray for one another, that you may be healed and restored. The heartfelt and persistent prayer of a righteous man (believer) can accomplish much [when put into action and made effective by God—it is dynamic and can have tremendous power."

- The scripture tells us in Ephesians 6:18 (NIV), "And pray in the Spirit on all occasions with all kinds of prayers and requests. . . ."

We should rejoice always and pray always. We should pray in the good times and bad times. We should pray during times of layoffs, financial stress, and when you feel burdened. During promotions and demotions, we should pray. During sickness and in health, we should pray. For better or for worse, we should pray.

My wife and I are always in a posture of prayer. When my wife's mother died suddenly, we were already in prayer. When her father was sick and later died, we were already in a posture of prayer. When my mother passed away from a long-term illness, we were praying. When our son was choking in the womb, we were already praying. When he had difficulties in school, we were in prayer. When my brother had a stroke, we were already praying. When my daughter and boyfriend decided to get married, we were definitely praying. When I ended up in the hospital unexpectedly, we were already praying.

When we had unexpected expenses like a broken-down car, a flooded basement, or appliances breaking down, we were already in prayer. Also, when we had some unexpected money come our way, we did not start praying, but instead we were already praying and giving thanks.

When you and your spouse pray, you should pray with purpose.

Here are the things you should purposely pray for.

You should purposely pray for peace. Philippians 4:7 (AMP) states, **"And the peace of God [that peace which reassures the heart, that peace] which transcends all understanding, [that peace which] stands guard over your hearts and your minds in Christ Jesus [is yours]."**

When the storms of life rock your marriage, call on the name of Jesus and ask him, "Do you not care that this marriage is about to sink? Lord we need your help." Watch the Lord stand up in your marriage and say, "Peace, be still."

Ask for peace that transcends all understating. When other couples are breaking up over cloudy days, pray that the Lord will grant your marriage peace while going through the middle of hurricane, pray for the peace that the Lord will bring your marriage safely to shore.

When you pray, you should pray for compassion. Pray Ephesians 4:32 (AMP), **"Be kind and helpful to one another, tender-hearted [compassionate, understanding], forgiving one another [readily and freely], just as God in Christ also forgave you."**

It is interesting how many people are kind and compassionate to total strangers but mean and disrespectful to their own spouse. It is just baffling how people treat people they meet once better than the person they see 365 days a year. Couples should pray for compassion. When you do not understand each other, pray for compassion to forgive your spouse when she/he wrongs you.

When you pray, you should pray for unity. Pray Colossians 3:14 (AMP), **"Beyond all these things put on and wrap yourselves in [unselfish] love, which is the perfect bond of unity [for everything is bound together in agreement when each one seeks the best for others]."**

Pray that you and your wife will be on the same page. You might not agree about everything but be united in a way that when you do not agree, it does not separate your love for each other.

Pray that you will be united in the handling of your finances, united in how to deal with your children, and united in where and when you should praise and worship.

Pray that you will be united dealing with extended family, that nothing should come between you and your spouse, and that neither your momma, daddy, nor your children can separate you.

Pray that you will be united in all aspects of your marriage, whether physically (I'll talk more about this in a later chapter) emotionally, or socially, talk with one another, spiritually support each other, and believe the same things that are in the scriptures.

Pray for complete unity that if your spouse decides to leave you, tell your spouse that you are going with him/her because you are one.

When you pray, pray for wisdom.

"Do not turn away from her (Wisdom) and she will guard and protect you; Love her, and she will watch over you. The beginning is: Get [skillful and godly] wisdom [it is preeminent]! And with all your acquiring, get understanding [actively seek spiritual discernment, mature comprehension, and logical interpretation]." Proverbs 4:6-7 (AMP)

The first step in living as husband in wife "Till Death Do You Part" is to Pray Every Day.

The second step to a lasting marriage is to Praise and Worship every week.

Let us examine this second step in more detail in the next chapter.

IV
PRAISE & WORSHIP TOGETHER

The marriage that praises and worships together, stays together. The second step in having a marriage that lasts "till death" would be to praise and worship together weekly. Since my wife and I married, I can count on one hand the times we did not praise and worship God together at a Sunday service. The marriage that prays tighter, stays tighter; also, the marriage that praises and worships God tighter, stays tighter.

What people fail to realize is that having a personal relationship with Jesus glues the marriage together, and it's important in a marriage to regularly praise and worship the keeper of the soul, who also is the keeper of your marriage. Attending praise and worship is not just a good suggestion, but it is also God's will for all believers.

The scriptures encourage us to praise and worship God in Hebrews 10:25 (NKJV), **"not forsaking the assembling of ourselves together, as is the manner of some, but exhorting one another, and so much the more as you see the Day approaching."**

When we read the above scripture, we think it is only talking about the significance of going to church, but we forget about the preceding verse

Hebrews 10:24 (NKJV) that says, **"And let us consider one another in order to stir up love and good works."**

Coming together in praise and worship with your spouse will stir up love and good works for God and for your spouse. If you truly love your spouse, praising and worshiping the God who brought you together is a demonstration of that love.

Collective praise and worship in a house of worship is the place where couples can come together to love one another and demonstrate good works.

The truths that couples can learn together in a church setting will also benefit the marriage. The scripture from the New King James Version (NKJV) offers these directions:

- 1 John 4:12 tells us to **"love one another."**
- Hebrews 3:13 tells us to **"exhort one another."**
- Galatians 5:13 tells us to **"serve one another."**
- Romans 15:14 tells us to **"admonish one another."**
- Romans 12:10 tells us to **"be devoted to one another"** and **"give preference to one another in honor."**
- Ephesians 4:32 tells us to **"be kind to one another, tenderhearted, forgiving one another, even as God in Christ forgave you."**

If these truths are good for the church body, it is even more beneficial to the marriage covenant. Attending church as a couple is the ideal place to help your marriage grow. Church is the place you can go to reinforce your commitment to God and to each other. Going to a spa will not do it. Going shopping together will not do it. Going out to a restaurant together or to see a movie will not do it. Only going to an agreed-upon worship location where you can praise and worship the creator of the marriage will keep your marriage grounded and on course.

There were times due to weather or other reasons we stayed at home and could not attend the praise and worship service in person, but that didn't deter us, because we would just praise and worship at home. We would sing songs, testify, and read scriptures, and I would preach a sermon, just as if we were in a church building. We did this because it was in our nature; it is what we have become. It is unnatural for us not to praise and worship God together. For us, praising and worshiping God is more than a nice thing to do, but it's something we learned that we must do.

I grew up in the church. My parents attended church on a regular basis, and they took all their six children to church. Attending church was not optional. As a child, I didn't attend church because I wanted to attend. I attended church because my parents said, "If you live in our house, if you eat the food we buy, and the clothes we bought, you are going to church."

My parents took seriously Joshua 24:15 (NKJV), **"But as for me and my household, we will serve the Lord."**

When my wife and I got married, my job moved us 3,000 miles away to California. In California, we did not have any friends or family. All we had was each other, and I found us, or rather the Lord found us, a church we should attend. We started attending New Sweet Home (NSH), Church of God in Christ (or COGIC) in East Palo Alto, California, on a regular basis. At that time, Superintendent AC Macklin was the pastor.

We spent the majority of our time in church. I look back now and see the necessity of this for our spiritual and martial growth. My wife and I joke now that we did not have time to start a family because all our waking hours were spent in the church.

In this church, we saw examples of godly marriages. We saw godly couples praising and worshiping God together with no shame. We saw godly couples serving in the church together, and we saw godly couples giving of their time, talents, and treasures unto the Lord.

We saw couples loving on each other and loving on God. We needed to see this early in our marriage; we needed to see that praising and worshiping and serving God as a couple works.

Seeing this was such an encouragement, given the fact that many Christian couples and non-Christian couples end up in divorce court. The examples of these couples showed us that we can make it, with the help of the Lord.

This church believed in praising and worshiping the Lord. They took praise and worship to another level. They were serious about their praise. I came from a Pentecostal background; I've seen shouting and dancing, speaking in tongues, hour-long praise services, but I never had seen praise and worship like at NSH COGIC. This church took praise and worship to an intensity I had never seen before. They were serious about their praise.

My wife came from a United Methodist background, so she wasn't accustomed to such an outward expression of praise and worship, but after a few services, she quickly caught on.

Attending and participating in praise and worship was not a burden for us, but a blessing. If you get to a point in your marriage that you do not enjoy getting up and praising our God, you should examine yourself.

Praise and worship at church was the highlight and still is the highlight of our week. Yes, we pray and study the Word throughout the week, but each Sunday morning we come together and uplift the name of Jesus together. There is no greater joy than to being in accord with your faith.

My wife and I learned to praise and worship God together without reservation. There is no shame in our praise. Once you get on the same page in your praise and worship, all other troubles seem like they are not such a big deal.

In other words, when trouble comes your way throughout the week, you can look forward to coming together to praise your way through.

We can praise and worship freely because we know what God has done for us as a couple. Jesus brought us out of sin and shame. He brought us out of the practice of sin, the power of sin, the punishment of sin, and the very presence of sin. That is why we praise Him. That is why we worship Him.

Praise is not foreign to us. As the songwriter William Murphy sings, "Praise Is What I Do."[13]

As I mentioned before, the church we attended when we first got married loved to praise the Lord. Not only did they love to praise the Lord, but they also loved to preach the Gospel, and they loved to teach the word of God to the people of God.

These lessons were important not just because we were a newly married couple, but we were new in our relationship with Christ. As new creatures in Christ, we needed sound doctrine to ground us in our faith and to sustain our marriage.

Pastor AC Macklin and the NSH COGIC family taught us this. Early in our marriage, we were regular attendees at weekly choir rehearsals, Wednesday Bible study, Friday night "Power Night" service, Sunday school, Sunday morning worship, and Sunday afternoon worship. We also attended any conference and marriage workshops that were available.

We were hungry for the word of God. Jesus said in Matthew 5:6 (NKJV), **"Blessed are those who hunger and thirst for righteousness, for they shall be filled."** This was true for us. We were truly hungry and thirsty, and we were unquestionably filled with praise and worship every single week of the year. That is what we did, and that is what we do.

Many couples attend separate churches for different reasons. Some attend different churches due to a desire for a different worship style. You may want shouting and dancing while your spouse prefers a more restrained worship style. You may have family ties and traditions with a particular church. However, if possible, it's best to attend the same church to worship together. The scripture tells us in Genesis 2:24, **that God created man and woman to be one flesh.** There is a unity in marriage that is unique and holy.

If possible, husband and wife should be united in all things, including where to praise and worship God. If the church is a Bible-believing church, a church that believes in the essentials of the Gospel and the basic doctrines of Christianity in dealing with God, Christ, sin, and salvation, the couple should pray to find the best church in which they could raise their family in the appropriate fear and admonition of the Lord.

In the early church, families praised and worshiped together. If there is an ongoing debate about where to worship, the husband as the spiritual head of the family should take the lead and make the final decision. The husband should stand up and say we shall worship at such-and-such church.

If your spouse is also a believer, he/she is more than just your spouse; he/she is your brother/sister in Christ. That means you have a double blessing, spending time with them here on Earth in praise and worship and seeing them again in eternity. We will spend more time with this person.

I challenge any married couple to try for three months to spend time weekly in praise and worship and see that it will make a difference in your marriage. Just try it and see how God will bring you closer to Him and closer to each other.

The first step in having a marriage that lasts until "death do you part" is to pray every day. The second step is to praise and worship every week. The third step is to play every month.

Let us examine this third step in more detail in the next chapter.

Let us Play.

V

PLAY TOGETHER

The marriage that plays together, stays together. When we hear "play," what comes to mind? When I hear play, I envision children playing on the playground — sliding down the slides, swinging joyfully on the swings, hanging off the monkey bars, playing tag, jumping rope, riding bikes. In other words, when I hear "play" I hear fun.

When was the last time you had fun with your spouse? I am talking about just enjoying one another without looking at the clock or looking at a bill.

The Bible says in Ecclesiastes 9:9 (NKJV), **"Live joyfully with the wife whom you love all the days of your vain life which He has given you under the sun, all your days of vanity; for that *is* your portion in life, and in the labor which you perform under the sun."**

As mentioned in a previous chapter, the scripture says, "Enjoy your wife." It does not say enjoy your girlfriend, lover, sweetheart, or roommate. It says "wife." You should enjoy the wife that God has given you.

Husbands and wives should enjoy each other — enjoy cuddling, enjoy spending time with each other, enjoy having sex with one another. Yes, I said having sex. Sex in the bounds of a marriage covenant is not bad, but it's good and beneficial. You and your wife should regularly engage in sexual play for the benefit of the marriage.

Sex is God's special gift to a husband and wife within the exclusive bonds of marriage. In other words, sex is made only for a husband and wife. Any other sex outside of a husband-and-wife relationship is a sin, according to God's word.

Paul wrote about sexual relations between a husband and a wife.

"A husband should satisfy his wife's needs. And a wife should satisfy her husband's needs. ⁴ The wife's body does not belong only to her. It also belongs to her husband. In the same way, the husband's body does not belong only to him. It also belongs to his wife. ⁵ You shouldn't stop giving yourselves to each other. You might possibly do this when you both agree to it. And you should only agree to it to give yourselves time to pray. Then you should come together again. In that way, Satan will not tempt you when you can't control yourselves." (1 Corinthians 7:3-5, NIrV)

Also, Solomon wrote about how to interact sexually with your wife.

"Drink water from your own well.
　Drink running water from your own spring.
Should your springs pour out into the streets?
　Should your streams of water pour out in public places?
No! Let them belong to you alone.
　Never share them with strangers.
May your fountain be blessed.
　May the wife you married when you were young make you happy.
She is like a loving doe, a graceful deer.
　May her breasts always satisfy you.
　May you always be captured by her love."
　(Proverbs 5:15-19, NIrV)

These scriptures are self-explanatory; they do not need any commentary. The word of God is plain regarding how husbands and wives should interact sexually. It speaks for itself. As a husband and wife, you should do as the songwriter Marvin Gaye sings, "Let's Get It On."[14]

This is what the scriptures have to say about sexual play in marriage.

However, having sex should not be the only thing you should do to institute "play" within your marriage. If you have sex every day, that is only a few minutes for some, or an hour or more for others, out of the entire day. What are you doing for the rest of the hours in the day?

You should adapt playful adventures — play dates with your spouse. You should always be dating in your marriage. One of my divorced friends mentioned to me that one thing that he wishes he would have done differently in his first marriage was to "never stop dating his wife." In other words, your marriage is done if you stop dating.

Continuing dating your spouse will keep your marriage fresh and new. It will break up the monotony of the everyday life. It will keep the fun and romance in the marriage. It will reinforce to each other important messages, like I still love you, even when you gain a few pounds after having children. I still love you even when you try to cover up the gray. I still love you even when you don't take out the trash, nor cook like my mother.

Do not stop dating. Dating is a sign that you still do love your husband or wife. How do you love your spouse? Well, love is an action word; we must show that we love one another.

God showed that he loved us by sending his son to die for us. He put his love into action.

Paul said in Ephesians 5:28-29 (NIV), **"In this same way, husbands ought to love their wives as their own bodies. He who loves his wife loves himself.** After all, no one ever hated their own body, but they feed and care for their body, just as Christ does the church."

Just as Christ loved the church is how we should love our wives. How did he love the church? He loved the church by caring and feeding the church. He took care of the church as we should take care of our wives, by showing love in concrete, practical ways.

The wife should not have to guess if her husband loves her. She should know by what he does more than what he says.

Both husbands and wives must act out their love for one another. Now, what does this look like? How do we demonstrate love?

The scriptures tell us what love looks like.

"Love is patient, love is kind. It does not envy, it does not boast, it is not proud. It does not dishonor others, it is not self-seeking, it is not easily angered, it keeps no record of wrongs. Love does not delight in evil but rejoices with the truth. It always protects, always trusts, always hopes, always perseveres. Love never fails. (1 Corinthians 13:4-8 (NIV)
That's what love looks like.

Each month, my wife and I set aside some time to show our love for each other and just play. We set aside time to visibly showcase our love for each other. This time is scheduled and is non-negotiable. Nothing unless there were an emergency would stop us from spending this time together.

We schedule time to play. With us both being busy on our jobs, with our children, and with the church, if we didn't schedule time to "play," it would not happen.

It is good to spend time with the one you love, having no other expectations other than just being with one another. I set aside money in the budget specifically for our dates. So when we go out, money is not a problem because I have prepared for it in the budget.

If I was planning a huge getaway out of town, I made sure to put extra money in the budget to cover the expenses. When we went out, I did not want my wife to be concerned about the cost because this was our time together and our time together was priceless (well, priceless within the budget).

It's good to spend time and money with someone where there are no strings attached. My wife and I just enjoy being with one another, letting down our hair and just being ourselves. My wife has seen me at my worst and at my best, and she still loves me. That's why we schedule play, because we are more than just husband and wife. We are more than just life partners and we are more than lovers, we are friends. My wife is my best friend and as friends, we enjoy spending time with one another.

"There are 'friends' who destroy each other, but a real friend sticks closer than a brother." (Proverbs 18:24, (NLT)

Someone once said, "A friend is someone who steps in when everyone else steps out." My wife has been in step with me from Day One, when we got married. I'm truly blessed. As friends, we like to be together and share our life together.

The scripture tells us, **"*Let* nothing *be done* through selfish ambition or conceit, but in lowliness of mind let each esteem others better than himself. Let each of you look out not only for his own interests, but also for the interests of others.** (Philippians 2:3-4) (NKJV)

This is the time in which we can look out for the interest of the other and love on the other through play.

When we schedule play, at times it is as simple as a movie and dinner, and at other times, it is an elaborate getaway out of town. During the COVID-19 pandemic, we could not go anywhere because all the entertainment places were closed. Even though there was no place to go, we still planned a date. What did we do? On one date, we hopped in our car and drove forty-five minutes to the farthest Walmart to shop. That was our date, driving, talking, and shopping.

Below are some ideas that go beyond the usual dinner and a movie.

I gathered all of the below information from the *For Your Marriage* website. This website has a lot of marriage resources to "help couples at all stages of life to understand and live God's plan for happy, holy marriages by providing educational and spiritual resources."[15]

Many of these ideas involve little or no cost. These are play activities that are free, cheap, outdoorsy, or home dates. You select based on your spouse's personality, preferences, and budget.

Absolutely Free

- Grab some microwave popcorn and binge watch some 70s TV Sitcoms like *Happy Days*, *M*A*S*H*, *All in the Family*, *Sanford and Son*, *Taxi*, *WKRP in Cincinnati*, *The Brady Bunch*, *Gilligan's Island*, *The Jeffersons*, and *Good Times*. After each episode discuss how the 70s themes differ from today's themes.

- Try pitching a blow-up mattress in your backyard, snuggling together under a warm blanket while gazing up in the heavenlies counting the constellations together.

- Go to a public place like the local mall or a park and watch the people go by. Talk about if you were writing a book about them, what detail you would include (profession, family, lifestyle, etc.). Keep a few $1 bills in your hand to give to any homeless person you encounter. Ask them their name and ask if you could pray for them.

- Each spouse privately dresses up in a weird outfit from something in your closets (no need to buy anything — just use anything you have in your house). Then come together and put on some praise and dance music and dance all over the house.

- Gather a big pile of leaves together and jump and play in them like you are two little kids. Don't worry about being cute or sophisticated, just be free. If you don't have any leaves to rake, go find a friend or neighbor who does and volunteer to rake their leaves for them.

- Find a big empty church and meditate and pray together. Allow the Holy Spirit to speak to you. Share with each other your thoughts concerning any issues you are having in your marriage.

- Take turns having a "Servant's Night." Pick a night to "serve" your spouse. You can run her/his bath water. Wait on him/her hand and foot. Make his/her favorite meal.

- Try walking in your spouse's shoes for a day by reversing roles. If the husband normally takes out the trash, the wife will do this. If the wife normally cooks the dinner, the husband would do this. It's a way to better understand life from your spouse's viewpoint.

- Have a "gadget free" night. Turn off all of your cell phones, iPods, computers and just talk the entire evening or read a book together.

Cheap Dates
- Play a board game with your spouse. Find one of the classic games like: *Twister, Clue, Guess Who, Life, Sorry, Battleship, Monopoly, Scrabble, Candyland, Trivial Pursuit,* and *Risk.* Don't put a time limit on your play. Just play the night away.

- Play nine rounds of miniature golf without keeping score. Once each round of golf is complete, share with your spouse one reason why you love them.

- Play being a tourist for the day. Make-believe that you just arrived in your city and you want to visit all of the exciting places. Go to the museums, parks, and eat at local establishments, just like a tourist.

- Go to the beach and build a sandcastle together. You don't have to be an expert builder, just make something that is fun and exciting that both of you can laugh about,

- Plan a "Favorites Night" around your favorite food, clothes, games, sports, etc. Each spouse could choose a favorite activity which they then combine into one evening, or the wife could propose her favorite activities for one date and the husband plans the next date with his favorites.

- Ride a local metro train for the whole route. Get off at the end of the stop, and explore the area, have lunch/dinner and ride the metro back to your original location.

- Whenever there is a huge snowstorm, run outside and have snowball fight with each other, then make a huge snowman, take a picture together and post it on Facebook.

- Visit a local animal shelter together. Look at the names and history of the dog/cats. Talk about any pets you had as a child.

- Find a local bowling alley and do a bowling breakfast early in the morning. It's usually less crowded and you can have fun with each other if you don't take the game too seriously.

- Look through old photo albums and tell each other stories of your childhood and families. If you feel really energetic, make it a time to put all those loose photos in albums or on a disc. It is a big job, but your children will appreciate it one day.

- Go fishing together. Catching fish is not the point. The point is spending time to together and just talking while fishing, If you catch anything, take it home, clean it and cook it together.

- Visit a local thrift store. See who can buy the finest attire at the cheapest price. Take the outfits to cleaners and wear them the following week during a dinner outing.

- Do something to nurture your spiritual life. Read a devotion together and share how the Lord is speaking to you. Knock on neighbors' doors and ask them how you can pray for them. Go to a church where you are not a member and praise the Lord together.

- Visit your local zoo. Many zoos allow you to feed the animals or offer petting areas. Find something new about each animal and have a discussion about what it would be like to live in the land where the animal came from.

- Volunteer somewhere together — help at a nursing home or a soup kitchen, or clean up litter from a park or along your street. Pray a simple litany of thanks together, i.e., "For our family, we thank you, Lord. For a safe home, we thank you, Lord. For our health, we thank you, Lord. . . ."

Outdoorsy Dates

- Find the closest body of water and take a walk along a body of water at night. Pause and gaze at the light shimmering on the water. Throw small pebbles in the water and count the ripples.

- Do something silly that reminds you of your childhood. Play hide-and-go-seek, go to a fast-food establishment, buy a couple of large French fries and feed the fries to the birds that fly by.

- Look for a local secluded location and have an old-fashioned picnic. Lay out a tablecloth, some snacks or a meal, and play some music. Read some romantic poetry to each other.

- Take an early morning or evening bike ride together around your neighborhood. Stop whenever you feel the urge. It is not a race, just a time to discover together.

- During the fall, find a corn maze and wander through it. Nighttime is the most fun. Getting lost is part of the adventure. Ponder how your experience may mimic times in your life together when you felt lost, found each other, or found your way through a difficulty together.

- Take your spouse on a drive-by memory lane. Visit where you first met, visit the place where you had your first date, visit your first house, visit where you first kissed, visit the place where your children were born, visit a home of a person who meant something special to your marriage. Memories are priceless. In the next chapter I will detail our memory-lane experience.

At-Home Dates
- Curl up for an evening of reading. Find a book you both enjoy and take turns reading to each other. For fun you might want to randomly read a sentence from each of your respective books and see what bizarre combinations this makes.

- The Bible may not seem like a date book, but try sharing your favorite passage with each other. Do not have a favorite passage? Explore the Song of Songs together. Share what you find physically attractive about your spouse.

- During the dark of winter, make some light together. Build a fire in the fireplace. Do not have a fireplace? Light a whole bunch of candles in a grouping. Lay out a blanket and have an indoor picnic — or at least some popcorn.

- Rent a classic romantic move like *Casablanca, Sense and Sensibility, The Princess Bride*, etc.

- Rent a Christian romantic movie like *I Still Believe, Forever My Girl, Benevolence, Until Forever, Marriage Retreat*, etc.

These are some suggestions that you could implement this week. The key is starting and continuing on a regular basis. Based on your schedule you might want to do something weekly, biweekly, or monthly, but whatever you do, plan for it and don't allow anything other than an emergency to get in the way of having your date night together.

Also, when you are with your spouse, make sure you are fully there. Turn off your cell phone or put it on mute. Make sure your spouse has your undivided attention for the time that you are together.

The first step is to pray every day. The second step is to praise and worship every week. The third step is to play every month. The fourth step in having a marriage that lasts "Until Death Do Us Part" is to make the Promise & Celebrate.

Let us examine this fourth step in more detail in the next chapter.

Let's make the Promise & Celebrate.

VI

PROCLAIM THE PROMISE TOGETHER

The scripture says this in Ecclesiastes 3:1, 3-5 (NRSV):
> "For everything there is a season, and a time for every matter under heaven: . . .
> a time to kill, and a time to heal;
> a time to break down, and a time to build up;
> a time to weep, and a time to laugh;
> a time to mourn, and a time to dance;
> a time to throw away stones, and a time to gather stones together.
> a time to embrace, and a time to refrain from embracing."

In your marriage, you will experience trials and tribulations. You will experience emotional killings, breakdowns, weeping, mourning, and stone-throwing.

These things are certain to happen in our marriage. Since it is most certain that these things will occur, we must make a conscious and deliberate decision to heal, build up, laugh, dance, and gather stones together in the marriage.

A happy marriage does not just happen. If you do not do anything to make it a happy marriage, it won't be a happy marriage.

Each year on the anniversary of our wedding, my wife and I celebrate big time and make the promise again to stay together as husband and wife, till death, no matter what.

We make the promise once again to be lawfully wedded as husband and wife, to have and to hold, for **better** or for **worse**, for richer or for poorer, in sickness and in health, to love and to cherish, from this day forward until death do us part.

We promise that no matter what the year looked like, no matter what struggles we have been through or are currently going through, divorce is not an option. I told my wife if she decides to leave me, I am going with her. I am packing my bags to let her know wherever she is going, I am right behind her. I let her know that she cannot shake me out of this marriage.

As married couples, we make the promise on the wedding day, but many forget the same promise when things do not go the way they planned. But we should be promise keepers.

The scriptures talk about keeping promises.

> **"When a man makes a vow to the Lord, or swears an oath to bind himself by a pledge, he shall not break his word; he shall do according to all that proceeds out of his mouth."** (Numbers 30:2, (NRSV)

When you make a vow to get married, not only do you make a vow to your spouse, but most importantly, you make a vow to God. When you get to a point in your marriage in which you think that you can't keep the vow, don't run and find the best divorce attorney, instead talk with your spouse, talk to a marriage counselor, but most importantly, have a talk with God. God knows and understands what you are going through.

> **"I will not violate my covenant or alter the word that went forth from my lips."** (Psalm 89:34, (NRSV)

As a married couple, just keep your word to stay together. It may be hard, but stay there. If you hang in there and do some work, the chances are that you will be happier and more content in your life.

"Researchers also found that two-thirds of unhappily married spouses who stayed married reported that their marriages were happy five years later. In addition, the most unhappy marriages reported the most dramatic turnarounds: among those who rated their marriages as very unhappy, almost eight out of ten who avoided divorce were happily married five years later."[16]

Renew the promise and celebrate. Jesus said this in Matthew 5:37 (NRSV):

> **"Let your word be 'Yes, Yes' or 'No, No'; anything more than this comes from the evil one."**

We should let our word be our bond. If you say "yes" to your spouse, you should stick to it. I hear many people say, "I got a divorce, what should I do now?" Well, you can't go back in time, the past is the past, but you should make the resolution that from this day forward if you get married again, you would make the promise to stay with your current spouse for life.

You should make the promise and celebrate the promise each year you are married. You should make the anniversary of your promise a special day.

Each year we renew the promise and celebrate in a special way. Each year we would set aside some time to rekindle that marriage moment.

We have gone on cruises to the Bahamas and Bermuda to celebrate. We have traveled to NYC and other cites to celebrate, just to hang out and reminisce.

One of our favorite celebratory locations is Lancaster, Pennsylvania. Lancaster is best known for being the hub of Pennsylvania's Amish Country. We have been to this location five or six times. We love going to this location because it slows us down and just gives us time to stop and reflect on how blessed it is to be husband and wife.

We also have gone on elaborate dinner dates. One year, we even celebrated at the restaurant where we had our first Valentine's Date.

On this special day, you and your spouse should be in the business of making lasting celebratory memories together.

For our twenty-eighth wedding anniversary, I told my wife that I wanted to celebrate with her by spending the entire day going down our relationship memory lane.

So, I planned to revisit twelve locations that were pivotal in our relationship before and after marriage. These twelve locations made us who we are. We wanted to have a celebratory day of remembrance.

My personal friend Bishop Bobby Holmes once said, "All you need to praise God is a memory." Songwriter Rev. Clay Evans sang "I've Got a

Testimony."[17] We have a testimony of how the Lord has kept us together for all these years.

When friends and family members were breaking up, we were still together by the grace of God. It wasn't because I was such a great husband, or my wife was such a great wife (OK, she is a great wife), but God kept us together; that's why each year we celebrate what God has done in our life and we just want to be an example to many couples out there that with the help of the Lord, you can make it.

Rev. Paul Jones sung the song, "I Won't Complain."[18]

I would end that song not by saying, "I won't complain," but "I will celebrate" — celebrate what God has done for me and my wife.

So we had a day of celebration and remembrance. I wanted to make the promise memorial. Therefore, I selected twelve roses, twelve anniversary cards, and twelve locations that were memorable for both of us.

This is what our day of anniversary celebration looked like.

Celebrating Memory Lane #1 — Local Eating Out

We started the day by having breakfast at the local IHOP (International House of Pancakes) in Landover, Maryland. For many years, we use to celebrate our birthdays at Farrell's Ice Cream Parlour at Landover Mall. This is where we would just talk and eat all the ice cream we could stomach. We loved going to this place. The parlors had an early 1900s theme, with employees wearing period dress and straw boater hats, and each location featured a player piano. This was our spot until it closed in late 2010.

So on this memory-lane day, instead of going to our favorite spot, we went to an IHOP down the street from our favorite spot.

We spent the time reminiscing about how the Lord has been with us these twenty-eight years. It was so ironic that our server was named Brianna — the same name and spelling as our daughter. That brought back another memory of how the Lord has blessed us with two wonderful children, who love the Lord and their parents. We could not ask for anything better.

Celebrating Memory Lane #2 — Prince Georges Community College (PGCC)

After breakfast, we drove to the location where we first met, PGCC. I remember being introduced to her by my best friend, Verdell Williams. He walked into the student game room and said, "I would like for you to meet a friend of mine, Pam." I shook her hand and said, "Nice to meet you."

I was thinking in the back of my mind, how did my friend meet up with this beautiful woman? I knew my friend was pretty smooth and a lady's man, but when I saw him with Pam, I concluded that he was truly "The Man." Little did I know that this beautiful woman would one day be my wife.

Celebrating Memory Lane #3 — My Parent's Home

After visiting PGCC, we drove across the street to my parents' house, and we reminisced about how Pam became a part of the Ruffin family. Even before we became husband and wife, my parents loved Pam and she loved them.

My parents' house is where I learned how to become a good husband. Before my wife and I got married, many asked us if we were going to attend marriage counseling. Now, I strongly encourage marriage counseling for all couples. Counseling can give you the opportunity to talk out some of the issues that may come up in the marriage.

However, my response to marriage counseling was that I didn't desire any counseling because I had experienced twenty-six years of counseling from my parents. By my living at home for twenty-six years, they taught me through their actions how to act in a marriage covenant. They lived an honorable married life. They lived the life of forsaking all others and clinging to their spouse. Not once did my father have a sweetheart, a lover, or a friend on the side. He was totally devoted to my mother. He once gave me some marriage advice; he said when times get rough, sometimes it's best just to take a walk around the block. My mother was very strong-willed, but she never disrespected my father in public. If they ever had a disagreement, the children never heard or saw it. My parents walked the walk and talked the talk. They never preached at us, but they spoke clearly with their lives.

While dating, Pam and I spent many days hanging around my house. There was a time we brought home some Chinese food and came back to my parents' house to eat it, and my dog "Dino" came out of nowhere and grabbed Pam's egg roll and ran upstairs. Pam did not get mad. She just laughed. From that experience, I knew she was the perfect one for me. Yes, that is only one of many good memories at my parents' house.

Celebrating Memory Lane #4 — Bowie State University (BSU)

After leaving my parents' home, we drove to BSU. Both of us transferred there after leaving PGCC. At BSU, I commuted while Pam stayed on campus. BSU was very different from PGCC. At BSU we had ups and downs, mostly because of me. After joining a fraternity, I thought I was "The Man." However, she did not want to be with "The Man," she wanted a man who acted like a man but I was acting like a little boy in a man's body. Because of this, Pam rightly kicked me to the curb several times. But I was like the children of Israel. Each time I did her wrong, she kicked me to the curb, and eventually I would come back asking for forgiveness. I knew when I had a good thing.

Our trials and tribulations at BSU taught us the art of forgiveness. It taught us that two people can be different and disagree but still love each other. Our experiences taught us that without a Christ-centered relationship, you are bound to grow apart because of your selfishness. It taught us that both of us needed Christ in our lives. While at BSU, we built many memories.

Celebrating Memory Lane #5 — Mr. & Mrs. Gwyns' Gravesite

We drove from BSU to another memory, my wife's parents' gravesite. When we arrived at the gravesite, my wife had this look on her face that said, "I thought this supposed to be a happy day; why are we at a gravesite?" I brought my wife to her parents' gravesite to reminisce about how her parents were pivotal in our relationship and marriage. From day one, both of her parents loved me.

I remember first meeting her father. I was later told that Mr. Gwyn scared off a lot of would-be boyfriends. Mr. Gwyn was a "real man." He loved his wife and his family. He did not take any stuff. He told it like it was. He was truly old school.

When I first met him, he asked me if I was in school. I told him, "Yes, Mr. Gwyn, I'm studying at PGCC and majoring in Business Administration." (I didn't tell him that I was flunking out.)

He asked me, "Are you working?" I told him, "Yes, Mr. Gwyn I'm working at Hechinger Warehouse." (I didn't tell him it was a part-time gig driving a forklift.)

He asked me, "What church do you attend?" I told him, "Mr. Gwyn, I'm a proud member of First Community Church. My father is even the pastor." (I didn't tell him that the last time I read the Bible was on Sunday when the preacher told the congregation to turn to a particular scripture.)

I did not tell him that I spent more time in the club than the church. I did not tell him that I was sinning and grinning. I did not tell him that I loved his daughter's mind and beauty, but marriage was the furthest thing from my mind. I am glad I didn't tell him about the real me. If I did, I would be part of the "would-be" boyfriend club.

At the gravesite, we reminisced about her mother, and how she was beautiful like Pam. Mrs. Gwyn was very sophisticated and always looked her best when she went out. We ruminated about how her mother used to fall asleep while watching the TV. To this day, my wife does the same thing.

One thing that made me appreciate my wife's parents was that they stayed out of our business. When my wife was at home, she was "little Pam." When she got married, she was no longer "little Pam" but became "Ms. Ruffin." When we decided to move 3,000 miles away, they did not question our decision. They sent us away with their blessing. Some people talk about how their in-laws are "out-laws," however, that was not my case. I loved my in-laws and they loved me.

Celebrating Memory Lane #6 — Mr. & Mrs. Gwyns' Home

After we left Pam's parents' gravesite, we went by her parents' home. For seven years, I picked up my girlfriend at this home to go on dates. One time, we were going out to dinner and Pam came down the steps looking like Miss America. I was speechless because this was the first time I thought she was stunningly beautiful.

At this home, I remembered the discussions I'd had with her parents. I remembered the times when Pam was always running upstairs to get her father's slippers and recalled where I would always help my wife's father put up the Christmas tree. I also remembered the time I borrowed my father's lawnmower to cut their grass, but the lawnmower caught fire and

Mrs. Gwyn had to call the fire department before I burned down the house. Yes, we reminisced about the Gwyn house. This house was truly a home.

Celebrating Memory Lane #7 — Mother Ruffin's Gravesite

After leaving the Gwyn house, we kept moving down memory lane by visiting my mother's gravesite. My mother, Mother Barbara Ruffin, loved my wife as her own daughter. She saw that Pam had a sweet, innocent spirit. She saw that Pam came from a good family that taught her how to look and act like a lady. When we were dating and even after we got married, my wife and mother use to go on shopping trips together. One thing that my mother showed us was how to love God and people. She lived out her faith and was loved by many. She was an exemplary wife to my father.

Mother Ruffin was truly a Proverbs 31 (NRSV) woman who had these qualities:

1. Faith (Proverbs 31:26)
2. Marriage (Proverbs 31:11-12)
3. Mothering (Proverbs 31:28)
4. Health (Proverbs 31:14-15)
5. Service (Proverbs 31:12)
6. Finances (Proverbs 31:14)
7. Industry (Proverbs 31:13)
8. Homemaking (Proverbs 31:27)
9. Time (Proverbs 31:19)
10. Beauty (Proverbs 31:22)

When my father found my mother, he found a good thing, and he obtained favor from the Lord.

Celebrating Memory Lane #8 — First Date

When my wife and I started dating, I didn't have much money. I was just a college student living at home with a part-time job. So, when we went on our first date, I had to come up with a cheap, classy date. What I did was I picked up a cheap kite at Toys "R" Us and drove down to the National Mall in Washington, D.C., and tried to fly the kite with my girlfriend on our first date.

It was a big disappointment. One thing I forgot was that having wind was a necessity for flying a kite. There was no wind and the kite went nowhere, but it was not a total loss because we spent the time together laughing and enjoying being with one another. She did not laugh at my failure, but she laughed with me. From this experience, I knew I had a winner.

So on this twenty-eighth anniversary date, we went down to the mall again. This time the kite flew up in the air, and we laughed once again. We laughed at how it was over thirty years since we did this, and the joy and fun were still there.

Celebrating Memory Lane #9 — Dulles Airport Marriage Proposal

Next stop on our memory lane was Dulles International Airport, the place where I proposed to my beautiful, lovely, gorgeous girlfriend who later became my wife.

When I proposed to my wife, I did it in a way that she continues to talk about after all these years. Here is the story. You might want to reach for the tissues.

I was moving 3,000 miles to California and wanted to bring my then girlfriend but I did not just want her with me as my girlfriend, I wanted her with me as my wife. I do not know if it was the shame of shacking up, explaining to her parents and my parents that I was taking Pam 3,000 miles away, or that I just did not want to be alone. All I knew is that I wanted her to be with me as my wife.

I think most women, especially those in long-term relationships, would prefer to be a wife, rather than a girlfriend, a lover, or a sleep-mate. A spouse is the highest state of a relationship. Finally, I wanted to take Pam to the highest state of our relationship.

So while returning from house-hunting in California, I decided that I wanted to propose to my girlfriend when I returned to the D.C. area.

While in California, I had purchased a dozen red roses and one white rose to give to my girlfriend. While on the plane back to D.C., I informed the flight attendant that I was planning to propose to my girlfriend, and I wanted them to help me with the proposal.

I showed them a picture of my girlfriend and told them that my girlfriend would be waiting at the gate for me. (It was OK for this to happen back in the day.) I asked the flight attendants and pilots to give my girlfriend a red rose when they get off the plane.

So the plane landed at Washington Dulles International Airport and Pam was at the gate, waiting for me to depart. This was a huge 747 with over 500 passengers on board.

My girlfriend waited and waited for me to disembark from the plane, but I was nowhere to be found.

Eventually, a flight attendant came up to my girlfriend and asked her if her name was Pam. She responded, "yes," and the flight attendant gave her a red rose. Each flight attendant and even the pilots gave her a red rose. I was the last person off the plane. I walked off the plane with a white rose in my hand. I knelt down on one knee in the middle of Dulles International Airport, and asked her to be my wife.

With hundreds of well-wishers in attendance, she said, "Yes" and the place erupted in a round of applause. Now that is how we started the "promise" — with a celebration. We started with a celebration, and each year we continue with a celebration.

Celebrating Memory Lane #10 — First House

After spending a few years in California, we returned to the Washington, D.C., area. We started looking for a place to stay. We decided to have a house built in the Gainesville, Virginia, area. This was an ideal location for us because we were around forty miles away from family and friends. In other words, people could not just drop by, but they would need to contact us before coming over.

This was our first place we truly owned. We had a mortgage. Praise the Lord — we were homeowners. At this location, we quickly learned that as homeowners, other expenses come along — expenses like furniture, painting, and cutting the lawn. I learned how to be a handyman. I believed and still believe in trying to fix things myself before calling someone else to fix it for me. My family can attest to many blunders I have made posing as "Mr. Fix It."

Celebrating Memory Lane #11 — Second House

We drove to our second house, which was twenty minutes away from the first house. We had wanted more room and a backyard for our growing family. We had memories of our cookouts and interesting neighbors and experiences like my son running from the neighbor's dog, or a friend of our son running through our screen. We remembered my brother-in-law's father having the ceiling fall on his head.

Also, I became a better handyman by building a shed, and a good friend, Kenny G., helped me with the roof. Equally, we experienced the wind blowing an umbrella pole through the siding of our house into our dining room. Anyway, we loved living in the Virginia area. We were not considering leaving the house or area. We were going to stay there forever, until. . . .

Celebrating Memory Lane #12 — Third House

Until the Lord told us to move. When we returned to our current house, the memories came to us about how the Lord opened up a door for us to get this house. While in Virginia, my wife's father became sick, and he spent many days in the hospital.

We were going back and forth to his hospital and to our church, which was forty-five miles away. We spent a tremendous amount of time going back and forth, and we spent a considerable amount of time on the road. The Lord spoke to me and said it was time to move. I tried to debate with God, telling him about the excellent schools, parks, and stores in the Virginia area, and I told him about the excellent commute to my job. The Lord told me it was time to move.

At that time, housing prices were through the roof. The prices were so high that we knew that they had to come down sometime. We sold our house at a very high price. A week later, the bubble burst and the prices of homes went down. With the money we received from the sale of our house, we were able to buy a bigger house in Maryland. Look at God! Won't He do it? The Lord knew that the bubble was about to burst, and he wanted to bless us.

I should have trusted God more when he told us to move. God knows how to bless His children. The scriptures tell us this:

- Proverbs 3:5 (NKJV) — **"Trust in the L**ORD **with all your heart, And lean not on your own understanding;"**
- Romans 8:28 (NKJV) — **"And we know that all things work together for good to those who love God, to those who are the called according to *His* purpose."**

On this day we celebrated with multiple celebrations. When we arrived at our current house, we continued to celebrate with a huge banner, a cake, and balloons. We need to continue to celebrate.

Couples should celebrate as often as possible for all occasions. Celebrating your union as husband and wife should be the number one celebration as a couple. A wedding anniversary should be celebrated more extensively than your birthday. Why? Because you did not have anything to do with the decision to be born. You should celebrate it more than Valentine's Day. Why? Because if you are not married to the one you love, you cannot prove that you are totally committed to be with that person for the rest of your life. You should celebrate it more than any other holiday.

Pastor Kevin Carson gives the following, *"9 Reasons Why You Should Celebrate Wedding Anniversaries"*[19]:

1. Covenant Faithfulness.

Marriage is a lifelong covenant of companionship between a man and a woman, created in the image of God, which results in unity for the purpose of dominion under God. Each anniversary celebrates another year of covenant faithfulness — not perfection as a couple but faithfulness to a promise made with each other and God.

2. Powerful Grace.

Powerful grace, indeed! Every marriage thrives off of grace. Grace is the oil that keeps the marriage running. In God's kindness, he provides grace that is new every morning. This is the grace celebrated every anniversary.

3. Forgiveness in Christ.

A personal relationship with God begins with eternal forgiveness from God to the believer through the personal work of Jesus. Marriage creates a context where both spouses have the privilege and responsibility to forgive each other often. This is the forgiveness celebrated every anniversary.

4. Commitment to Glorifying God.

God desires for all followers to glorify Him daily in everything. **"Therefore, whether you eat or drink, or whatever you do, do all to the glory of God."** (1 Corinthians 10:31, NKJV) Marriage becomes the proving ground where these decisions are determined and demonstrated. This is the commitment to glorifying God that is celebrated every anniversary.

5. Progressive Sanctification.

Sanctification is a progressive work of God and man that makes us more and more free from sin and like Christ in our actual lives. Life's most significant process — progressive sanctification — takes place in the rich environment of marriage. Two sinners. One covenant. A life full of opportunities to grow in Christ together. This is the sanctification process celebrated every anniversary.

6. Lifelong Companions.

When we make our marriage vows, we begin making a life together — learning to love each other as we weld two individual lives together as one. We commit to each other as we commit to Christ. We recognize we are in this for life. It is not a blind chance but a deliberate choice. This is the lifelong companionship celebrated every anniversary.

7. God's Sovereignty.

Just as specifically as God gave Adam and Eve to each other, God uses our own personal choices to give us our spouses. As we choose each other on our wedding day, God providentially and lovingly works out His plan. God uses the occasion of our marriage to provide for us our lifelong companion. This is the sovereignty of God celebrated every anniversary.

8. Building and Celebrating Memories.

Each anniversary means another calendar year has transpired. Twelve months. Four seasons. Good days. Not-so-good days. Sometimes horrific days. Good times. Bad times. Holidays. Workdays. Weekends. Vacations. Life. Memories have been built as days have been lived. The contours of life change as these moments apply pressure, make impressions, and provide wrinkles. This is building and celebrating of memories celebrated every anniversary.

9. Continued Love.

From the first conversations, through the length of the engagement, to the wedding day, love drives the process. Immature love changes to a mature love. Imperfect love remains imperfect but steadfast. This is the continued love celebrated every anniversary.

The fourth thing to do in order to live "till death do you part" as husband and wife is to celebrate the wedding promises every year. Do it loud and proud. Say it loudly to your spouse and the world, "I'm married and I'm proud to be married." Show your spouse and the world that you will stay together "Till Death Do You Part."

VII

TILL DEATH DO US PART

What I have outlined in this book may seem simple; however, if you incorporate these four principles into your marriage, they could profoundly make a lasting and significant impact on your marriage.

If you . . .

- Pray Every Day
- Praise & Worship God Together Every Week
- Play Together Every Month
- Promise & Celebrate Every Year

. . . you too will be able to stay together and to say to your spouse after forty, fifty, sixty years, "I still make the promise to you to be my lawfully wedded spouse, to have and to hold, from this day forward, for better or for worse, for richer or for poorer, in sickness and in health, to love and to cherish, from this day forward until death do us part."

ABOUT THE AUTHOR

Patrick Ruffin is the co-pastor of First Community Church in Bowie, Maryland. He is married to his lovely wife, Pamela, and they have two grown children. He loves God, his wife, and his family.

Endnotes

1   Schlesman, Sue. "10 Hidden Consequences of Divorce (Especially If You Have Kids)." Crosswalk.Com, 17 Jan. 2019, www.crosswalk.com/family/marriage/divorce-and-remarriage/10-hidden-consequences-of-divorce-especially-if-you-have-kids.html.

2   Keller, Tim. "Men, You'll Never Be a Good Groom to Your Wife Unless You're First a Good Bride to Jesus. - Christian Marriage Quotes." Christian Marriage Quotes - The World's Most Comprehensive Resource for Gospel-Centered Marriage Inspiration, 20 Sept. 2020, christianmarriagequotes.com/2358-men-youll-never-be-a-good-groom-to-your-wife-unless-youre-first-a-good-bride-to-jesus.

3   Stanton, Glenn. "Divorce Rate in the Church – As High as the World?" Focus on the Family, 23 June 2020, www.focusonthefamily.com/marriage/divorce-rate-in-the-church-as-high-as-the-world.

4   "Glorify God Together: A Marriage of Purpose." ChristianBible-Studies.Com | Transformed by the Truth, www.christianitytoday.com/biblestudies/g/glorify-god-together-marriage-of-purpose.html. Accessed 30 Mar. 2021.

5   Kloster, Julie. Glorify God Together: a Marriage of Purpose: Single Session Bible Study: How Can Our Marriage Be in One Accord, so That with One Heart and Voice We Glorify God? (Marriage Partnership Studies Book 4). Christianity Today, 2015.

6   Geiger, A., and Gretchen Livingston. "8 Facts About Love and Marriage in America." Pew Research Center, 13 Feb. 2019, www.pewresearch.org/fact-tank/2019/02/13/8-facts-about-love-and-marriage.

7   Beyoncé, "Single Ladies (Put a Ring on It)", track 1 (disc 2) on *I Am... Sasha Fierce*, Columbia, 2008, compact disc.

8   Stetzer, Ed. "Marriage, Divorce, and the Church: What Do the Stats Say, and Can Marriage Be Happy?" The Exchange | A Blog by Ed Stetzer, 14 Feb. 2014, www.christianitytoday.com/edstetzer/2014/february/marriage-divorce-and-body-of-christ-what-do-stats-say-and-c.html.

9   Strand, Paul. "Divorce Shocker: Most Marriages Do Make It." CBN News, 14 Feb. 2019, cmsedit.cbn.com/cbnnews/us/2014/May/Divorce-Shocker-Most-Marriages-Do-Make-It.

10   Shmerling, Robert H. "The Health Advantages of Marriage." Harvard Health Blog, 24 June 2020, www.health.harvard.edu/blog/the-health-advantages-of-marriage-2016113010667.

11   Curtin, Sally, and Betzaida Tejada-Vera. "Products - Health E Stats - Mortality Among Adults Aged 25 and Over by Marital Status: United States, 2010–2017." Centers for Disease Control and Prevention, 10 Oct. 2019, www.cdc.gov/nchs/data/hestat/mortality/mortality_marital_status_10_17.htm.

12   Luscombe, Belinda. "A Guy Read 50 Years' Worth of Relationship Studies. He Came Up With 17 Strategies." Time, 6 Sept. 2017, time.com/4927173/relationships-strategies-studies.

13   William Murphy, "Praise Is What I Do", track 11 (disc 2) on *Praise Is What I Do*, Kingdom, 2000, compact disc.

14   Marvin Gaye, "Let's Get It On", track 1 on *Let's Get It On*, Hitsville U.S.A, 1973, vinyl record.

15   Carson, Kevin. "9 Reasons Why to Celebrate Wedding Anniversaries." KevinCarson.Com, 28 June 2017, kevincarson.com/2017/06/17/9-reasons-why-to-celebrate-wedding-anniversaries.

16   Waite, Linda, et al. "Does Divorce Make People Happy?" USA Today, 11 July 2002, www.fact.on.ca/news/news0207/ut02071a.htm.

17   Clay Evans, "I've Got a Testimony", track 6 on *I've Got a Testimony*, Meek Records, 1995, compact disc.

18   Rev. Paul Jones, "I Won't Complain", track 4 on *I Won't Complain*, Pure Platinum, 2010, compact disc.

19   Carson, Kevin. "9 Reasons Why to Celebrate Wedding Anniversaries." KevinCarson.Com, 28 June 2017, kevincarson.com/2017/06/17/9-reasons-why-to-celebrate-wedding-anniversaries.

www.ingramcontent.com/pod-product-compliance
Lightning Source LLC
LaVergne TN
LVHW011851060526
838200LV00054B/4279